AMERICAN PRESIDENTS

THEODORE ROOSEVELT

INDIA JAMES

NORWOOD HOUSE PRESS

Cataloging-in-Publication Data

Names: James, India.
Title: Theodore Roosevelt / India James.
Description: Buffalo, NY : Norwood House Press, 2027. | Series: American presidents | Includes glossary and index.
Identifiers: ISBN 9781978579965 (pbk.) | ISBN 9781978579972 (library bound) | ISBN 9781978579989 (ebook)
Subjects: LCSH: Roosevelt, Theodore, 1858-1919--Juvenile literature. | Presidents--United States--Biography--Juvenile literature. | Legislators--United States--Biography--Juvenile literature.
Classification: LCC E757. J36 2027 | DDC 973.911092--dc23

Published in 2027 by
Norwood House Press
2544 Clinton Street
Buffalo, NY 14224

Designer: Rhea Magaro
Editor: Kim Thompson

Photo credits: Cover, pp. 1, 5-9, 11-19 Library of Congress; p. 21 Shutterstock.com;

Printed in the United States of America

CPSIA compliance information: Batch #CSNHP27: For further information contact Norwood House Press at 1-800-237-9932.

TABLE OF CONTENTS

Early Years....4

Building a Career....8

Presidency....12

Later Life....18

Glossary....22

Thinking Questions....23

Index....24

About the Author....24

Early Years

Theodore Roosevelt Jr. was born on October 27, 1858. He lived with his mother, father, two sisters, and a brother. The wealthy family had this big house in New York City.

28

Theodore had **asthma** and was sick a lot of the time when he was a kid. His father told him that exercise would make him strong. Theodore spent many hours boxing, riding horses, and playing outside. These activities helped him stay healthy.

Building a Career

Theodore went to Harvard University, where he studied law. People there called him "Teddy." The nickname stuck.

Theodore became a **politician**. He was elected to the New York state **legislature** in 1881. He became a leader in government.

Theodore married Alice Hathaway Lee in 1880, and they had one daughter. Alice died in 1884. In 1886, Theodore married Edith Kermit Carow. Theodore and Edith had five children together.

The Spanish-American War started in 1898. Theodore organized a group to fight in the war. It was made up of cowboys, football players, police officers, and Native Americans. They were called the Rough Riders. They became famous for winning battles.

Presidency

Theodore was well-known after the war. He became **governor** of New York in 1899.

The next year, he was chosen by William McKinley to be the U.S. vice president. President McKinley died in 1901. Then, Theodore became the 26th president of the United States.

As president, Theodore was known for helping workers. He broke up big companies called **trusts** and made them into smaller companies. This increased competition between businesses. It helped workers earn more money. People called him a **trustbuster**.

President Roosevelt loved nature and spent a lot of time in the wilderness. He wanted to **preserve** the nation's wild areas. He started 150 national forests and five national parks.

Later Life

Theodore Roosevelt served two **terms** as president. He left the White House, but he missed it.

A few years later, he ran for president again. This time, he lost the election to Woodrow Wilson.

Theodore died on January 6, 1919. People remember him for helping workers. They remember his love of nature and animals, including bears. Teddy bears are named after him!

Glossary

asthma (AZ-muh): a lung disease that makes it difficult to breathe

governor (GUHV-ur-nur): the elected leader of a U.S. state

legislature (LEJ-is-lay-chur): a group of people who have the power to make or change laws for a state or country

politician (pah-li-TISH-uhn): a person elected or chosen to hold a government office

preserve (pri-ZURV): to protect and keep safe

terms (turmz): definite or set periods of time; American presidents are elected to terms that last four years

trustbuster (TRUHST-bus-tur): a politician who splits big companies into smaller companies so there is more competition between businesses, resulting in lower prices and higher wages

trusts (truhsts): large businesses that control an entire industry or a large part of the economy; monopolies

Thinking Questions

1. What health problem did Theodore have?

2. In what state did Theodore serve as a legislator and governor?

3. Who were the Rough Riders?

4. How did Theodore become a U.S. president?

5. What stuffed animal is named after Theodore Roosevelt? Why?

Index

asthma 6

Harvard University 8

McKinley, William 13

national parks 17

New York 4, 8, 12

Rough Riders 10

teddy bears 20

trustbuster 14

About the Author

India James writes about science, technology, math, and history for young readers. She loves learning new things while writing books. India lives in Ohio with her family.